Jennifer Gallagher

# Adventure on the Hoe



Cornelsen

**Cornelsen English Library**

**Jennifer Gallagher · Adventure on the Hoe**

**Verlagsredaktion**
Mara Leibowitz

**Umschlaggestaltung**
Cornelsen Verlag Design

**Titelbild**
Trevor Burrows Photography, Plymouth

**Illustration**
www.davidnorman.com, Meerbusch

**Gestaltung & technische Umsetzung**
Annika Preyhs für Buchgestaltung+, Berlin

Passende Arbeitsblätter und weitere Hilfen zu diesem Titel gibt es unter:
www.cornelsen.de/cel

**www.cornelsen.de**

1. Auflage, 1. Druck 2012

Alle Drucke dieser Auflage sind inhaltlich unverändert und können im Unterricht nebeneinander verwendet werden.



Druck: H. Heenemann, Berlin

ISBN 978-3-06-032552-8

Inhalt gedruckt auf säurefreiem Papier aus nachhaltiger Forstwirtschaft.

# Contents

# Chapter 1

'OK, thanks class. It's time to go home,' said Ms Lee. 'See you tomorrow.'

The kids in class 7Y at Eggbuckland Community College put their books in their school bags.

'Hurray, just one more day at Eggy and then it's the weekend,' Ellie said to Berry. Then they walked out of the classroom.

'Yes,' said Berry. 'Do you have plans for the weekend?'

'No, I don't,' said Ellie. 'I like weekends but nothing much happens. What about you?'

'I don't have any plans. Maybe we can meet Luca and Adam,' said Berry.

'That's a great idea. What can we do?' asked Ellie.

'Hmmm, we can go to the Aquarium,' said Berry.

'It's expensive,' said Ellie.

'Shopping at Drake Circus?' said Berry.

'That's a girl thing,' laughed Ellie.

'Yeah, you're right. I know! Let's have a picnic on the Hoe,' said Berry.

'Yeah, a picnic is a cool idea. Look! There's Adam and Luca. We can ask them about the picnic,' said Ellie. 'Hey, Adam, Luca, please come here. We have a question for you.'

'Hi guys. What's up?' asked Adam.

'Is it a question about our maths homework? I'm too tired to think about homework,' said Luca. 'Today was a really hard day at school and I want to go home.'

'No, don't worry. It's not a question about homework. It's a nice question,' laughed Berry. 'Do you want to have a picnic on the Hoe with us this weekend?'

'With your mum and dad?' asked Luca. 'Er … your parents are nice but …'

'That's OK, Luca. I like my parents but a picnic with them isn't much fun. It's boring,' laughed Berry. What about a picnic with me and Ellie? Maybe my dog Sam can come too.'

'Oh, that's different. Yeah, cool,' said Luca.

'What about you, Adam? Can you come?' Ellie asked.

'It sounds great. And I think your dog Sam is really cool. But can we have the picnic on Sunday?' asked Adam.

'What's the problem with Saturday?' asked Ellie.

'I can't come on Saturday because I have to work in the cafe. Saturdays are really busy,' said Adam.

'Sunday is better for me too,' said Berry. 'I sometimes have to help mum in the farm shop on Saturdays.'

'OK. Let's have our picnic on Sunday. We can all bring some food and drink,' said Ellie.

'What do we need?' asked Adam.

'Let's think about it this evening and talk about it at school tomorrow,' said Berry. 'My mum is outside in the car. She's waiting for me. She worries about me so I have to go now.'

'OK, that's a good plan,' said Ellie. 'See you tomorrow, Berry.'

'Bye, Berry,' said Luca and Adam.

'Bye, guys. Do your maths homework,' laughed Berry.

'I hate Maths,' said Luca to Adam. 'It's very difficult. And I hate homework. I want to ride my bike and have an adventure. I don't want to do homework.'

'Yeah, I know,' said Adam. 'But don't worry. I can come to your house now and help you.'

'That's really nice of you. Thanks,' said Luca.

'No problem,' said Adam. 'That's what friends are for.'

'Yes, Adam is right. Don't worry,' said Ellie. 'Do your homework first and then you can both think about what we need for our picnic.'

'OK. See you tomorrow Ellie,' said Adam.

'Bye, guys,' said Ellie.

'Bye,' said Luca.

The next day, the four friends met in the school canteen for lunch and talked more about the picnic.

'My parents are cool about it,' said Adam. 'I told them we want to do our homework together.'

'Ha, ha,' said Ellie. 'What about your parents Luca?'

'Yeah, it's cool with them,' said Luca.

'Great, so what can we bring for our picnic?' asked Berry. 'Can you make a list please, Ellie? Here's some paper.'

'OK,' said Ellie.

'We need lots of food,' said Luca. 'You know, sweets and crisps.'

'OK, but we need good food too,' said Berry. 'Fruit, that's good. I can bring fruit from the farm.'

'Luca is bringing crisps and sweets. I'm bringing fruit,' said Berry. 'What about you, Adam?'

'I can bring lots of sandwiches from the cafe,' answered Adam.

'Hey, we need something to drink too,' said Luca. 'Orange juice and water are good.'

'Yeah, your dog Sam needs lots of water,' said Adam to Berry.

'No problem,' said Berry. 'I can bring water and orange juice too.'

'And I can bring a big chocolate cake,' said Ellie. 'This all sounds really good. A picnic on the Hoe – cool!'

# Chapter 2

It was Sunday morning. Luca was at home in the kitchen and getting ready for the picnic. He put lots of crisps and sweets in his backpack. His little sister Grace watched him.

'What are you doing?' she asked. 'That's a lot of food. Are you going away for a long time?'

Luca laughed.

'Ha, ha. No,' he said. 'I need this food for a picnic with some friends from school.'

'I love picnics,' said Grace. 'Can I come?'

'Sorry, Grace,' said Luca. 'Maybe we can go for a picnic next weekend, OK?'

'OK,' said Grace. She wasn't happy.

Suddenly, Luca's mobile phone beeped. It was a text from Adam:

> Hi Luca, do U want 2 meet me at the harbour 4 ice cream in 40 mins? Then we can go to Hoe 2gether.

Luca sent a text message back:

> Cool. C U there!

Then Luca's dad came into the kitchen.

'Luca, can you buy me a newspaper when you go?' he asked. 'Here's some money.'

'No problem,' said Luca. 'Do you want the *Plymouth Herald?*'

'The *Herald* is fine. The London newspapers have a lot of reports about robberies and murders.'

'But robberies and murders are exciting, Dad. Nothing like that happens in Plymouth!' said Luca.

Luca's dad laughed. 'Have fun at your picnic, and don't come back too late.'

'Don't worry. Thanks, Dad. See you later,' said Luca.

About 50 minutes later, Adam was standing by the ice cream van at the harbour. He looked at his watch. Luca was late.

SCREECH!

'Hi, sorry I'm late,' said Luca as he stopped and got off his bike.

'Hi, Luca, are you OK?' asked Adam.

'Yeah, I wanted to ride through the shopping zone because it's quick,' said Luca. 'But Mayflower Street was closed.'

'Closed on a Sunday? Hmmm, do you know why?' asked Adam.

'I don't know. I didn't ask,' said Luca. 'There were lots of police cars there too.'

'That doesn't sound good,' said Adam. 'Well, maybe we can look for a report in the *Herald* tomorrow.'

'Oh, no!' said Luca. 'I forgot to buy the *Herald* for my dad.'

'Don't worry,' said Adam. 'Let's buy an ice cream. We have time before we meet Ellie and Berry on the Hoe.'

'Good idea,' said Luca.

The two boys went to the window of the ice cream van. Inside, the ice cream woman had the *Herald*.

'Excuse me,' said Adam. 'Can I have a small '99 Flake, please?'

The ice cream woman put her newspaper on her chair. 'Sure you can,' she said.

'And for me too, please,' said Luca.

The ice cream woman gave the boys their ice cream.

'That's four pounds, please,' she said. 'That's two pounds for you and two pounds for your friend.'

Suddenly, there was a loud noise over their heads.

'What's that?' Luca said to Adam as they both looked up.

'Wow, that's a police helicopter,' said Luca. 'Cool.'

'Yeah, it's coming from Mayflower Street and going to the Hoe,' said Adam. 'Come on! Let's hurry up. Maybe we can see something.'

The ice cream woman looked out of the van's window. 'Don't worry,' she said. 'It's just ...'

But before she finished her sentence, the boys were gone!

## Chapter 3

Ellie was first on the Hoe. There were some seagulls looking for food but there weren't many people. She walked to the lighthouse and the big wheel and then she saw a great place for the picnic. As she took a big chocolate cake out of her backpack, the police helicopter flew over the Hoe and the sea. Ellie looked up and saw the helicopter, then put the cake on the picnic blanket.

Then Adam and Luca arrived.

'Hi, guys,' said Ellie.

'Hi, Ellie, did you see the police helicopter?' Adam asked. He was excited.

'Yes, it was very loud,' said Ellie.

'We saw it from the harbour,' said Luca. He was excited too.

Luca talked to Ellie about all the police cars at the shopping centre and that Mayflower Street was closed.

'You live near the shopping centre. Do you know what's happening?' Adam asked Ellie.

'Well, my dad's new flat is there,' said Ellie, 'but I was at my mum's house so I took the bus here. I don't know what's happening at the shopping centre. Maybe we can read a report on it tomorrow in …'

'The *Herald*,' said Luca and Adam together. 'Yes, we know.' Then they both laughed.

'I don't know what's so funny,' said Ellie. 'What do you think about my cake?'

'Oh, cool,' said Adam.

He opened his backpack. 'Here are some sandwiches and scones from the cafe. There's cream and jam for the scones too.'

'Scones are my favourite,' said Luca. 'And here are some crisps and sweets.'

The two boys put their food next to Ellie's big chocolate cake.

'We have lots of food,' said Adam. 'Can I have some cake now?'

'Let's wait for Berry,' said Ellie. 'OK?'

'OK,' said Adam.

'Don't worry,' said Ellie. 'There she is. I can see her. And Sam is with her too.'

'Hurray,' said Adam. 'Soon we can eat!'

Berry's mum pushed Berry in her wheelchair. Sam ran to Ellie and wagged his tail.

'Hello Sam,' said Ellie. 'I'm happy to see you too.'

'Hi, Ellie,' said Berry. 'Sorry I'm a bit late. Some of the roads were closed.'

'Yeah, I know,' said Ellie. 'Hello, Mrs Donovan.'

'Hi, Ellie,' said Berry's mum. 'It's nice to see you.'

'I can push you now,' Ellie said to Berry.

'Thanks,' said Berry. 'Come and say hi to Luca and Adam, Mum. They're over there, I can see them.'

'OK, but I won't stay for long,' said Mrs Donovan.

Sam ran to Luca and Adam. Adam was really happy to see Sam. Sam was very happy to see Adam and to see the sandwiches and cake.

'Nice to see you all,' said Berry's mum. 'I must go now but phone me when you want to come home, Berry.'

'OK, Mum,' said Berry. 'Oh, we can take Sam for a walk later. Where is his lead?'

'I have it. Here you are. Don't take Sam near the cliff. It's very dangerous,' said Berry's mum.

At that moment, two police helicopters flew over the Hoe. For a second, Mrs Donovan and the kids looked up at it. But Sam didn't. He ate one of the sandwiches.

'Don't forget Sam's lead,' said Berry's mum.
'Don't worry, Mum,' said Berry.

'OK, see you later. Have fun!' said Berry's mum.

'Bye, Mrs Donovan,' said Luca and Adam.

'Bye, Mum,' said Berry.

'Can we eat now?' asked Adam. 'I'm very hungry.'

'Great idea,' said Berry. 'Here is some orange juice, some water for Sam and some fruit from the farm.'

'Er … thanks,' said Adam. 'But first, can I have some chocolate cake, please?'

All the kids laughed at Adam.

'Yes, let's eat before the seagulls find us and eat our food,' said Ellie.

'I don't like seagulls,' said Luca. 'They're loud and they all look the same.'

'But they aren't all the same,' said Berry. 'There are lots of different seagulls in the UK.'

'Really!' said Ellie.

'Yeah, I saw a really good film about seagulls on the TV last week,' said Berry.

'I think seagulls are OK,' said Ellie. 'They live here and they aren't dangerous.'

'No, not like the cliffs,' said Luca. Then he laughed.

Adam gave Sam a sandwich and Sam wagged his tail. He was happy and the kids were happy. They didn't hear the police sirens – the kids and Sam were enjoying their picnic.

## Chapter 4

'There's still a bit of chocolate cake. Do you want it, Adam?' asked Ellie. 'It's for you. And there are still some sandwiches and scones.'

'No, thanks,' said Adam.

'Is that a joke?' laughed Ellie.

Luca and Berry laughed too.

'No, I'm really, really full,' said Adam.

'It's stupid to take food back home,' said Ellie.

'No, it isn't,' said Berry.

'We can give it to the seagulls,' said Adam.

'Adam, what does it say over there?' asked Luca.

'Er ... It says "Don't feed the seagulls",' said Adam. 'But I don't understand why. Seagulls have to eat too, and we eat all their fish.'

'Hmm ... but seagulls can get very mean when people feed them,' said Berry.

'OK, you're right,' said Adam. 'They're a bit scary.'

'We can eat the other food later,' said Ellie.

'Good idea,' said Luca. 'So what can we do now?

'What about a game of frisbee?' said Ellie.

'Cool,' said Luca and Adam together.

'Sam loves frisbee and I do too,' said Berry 'But he's really good.'

'Sam is so cool,' said Adam. 'He's the coolest dog in the world!'

Ellie took the frisbee out of her backpack and Sam wagged his tail. She threw the frisbee and Sam ran and then caught it in his mouth.

'Wow, he's good,' said Luca.

'Bring it here, Sam,' said Berry.

Sam ran to Berry and she took the frisbee from him. Then she threw it to Luca. Sam ran to the frisbee but Luca caught it first and then he wanted to throw it to Adam. Adam was very near to the cliff.

'Be careful Luca!' shouted Ellie. 'There's a lot of wind so don't throw the frisbee too near to the cliff. Sam mustn't run too near them.'

'Don't worry!' shouted Adam.

Adam ran to a place that wasn't dangerous for Sam.

'Come on, Luca. Throw it!' shouted Adam.

'This is fun,' said Berry. 'Throw it to me, Adam!'

The kids played lots of frisbee and then they sat on the grass and had something to drink. Sam drank some water and then took the frisbee.

'No more frisbee, Sam,' said Berry.

'Can we take Sam for a walk now?' asked Adam.

'Good idea,' said Berry. 'We have to stay on the path. Can one of you push me? What do you think, guys?'

'Fine with me,' said Ellie.

'We can't take our bikes on a walk,' said Luca.

'No, but the bikes can stay here,' said Adam.

'OK,' said Luca.

When Berry put the dog lead on Sam, he wagged his tail.

'OK, let's go,' said Ellie. 'I can push you first, Berry.'

'Thanks,' said Berry. 'And Sam can help – he can pull me at the same time when I hold onto his lead. He's very strong.'

Five minutes later, the four kids and Sam were walking on the path next to the cliffs.

'There's lots of rubbish and old food here,' said Berry.

'Yeah, and in the bushes too,' said Ellie.

'There are lots of rubbish bins here on the Hoe,' said Berry. 'Why do people throw things on the grass?'

'I don't know,' said Ellie.

'Look down there,' said Luca. 'The Lido looks really small from up here.'

At that moment, a seagull flew over and down to the sea.

'I feel like that seagull,' said Adam. 'I want to fly and dive into the Lido.'

'What? And catch a fish?' laughed Ellie.

'I want to see a police helicopter, not seagulls,' said Luca.'

For a moment Adam was quiet. Then he said, 'Berry, can I take Sam on the lead now?'

'OK,' said Berry. 'But be careful. He's strong. Here, take the lead.'

'No problem,' said Adam. 'I'm strong too.'

The kids stopped walking for a moment. A seagull was in front of them on the path. It was eating a bit of old bread. Berry had Sam on the lead. But before Adam took Sam from Berry, the seagull ran with the bread into the bushes. Suddenly, Sam ran after the seagull and into the bushes too.

'Sam! Come here!' shouted Berry. 'Come here now!'

She shouted again. Adam, Luca and Ellie were very quiet. Sam didn't come back.

'Oh, no,' said Berry. 'The cliff!'

Please DON'T
FEED THE
SEAGULLS

## Chapter 5

For five minutes all the kids called Sam's name but they didn't see him and he didn't come back.

'Berry, I'm really sorry,' said Adam. 'That stupid seagull – I didn't know … it was all so quick.'

'Sam doesn't usually run after seagulls or any birds on the farm,' said Berry.

'We must do something,' said Ellie. 'We can't just wait here for Sam to come back. Maybe he's hurt.'

'Yeah, maybe he fell down the cliff,' said Luca.

Berry put her head in her hands. 'Oh, Sam,' she said.

Ellie hugged Berry.

'Maybe he's OK,' said Ellie. 'Maybe he's sitting down there and waiting.'

'Waiting? Waiting for what?' said Luca.

'Luca, you're a pain and not much help,' said Ellie.

'Er … OK … I'm sorry,' said Luca. 'I can get my bike and then go home and ask my brother to help us.'

'There's no time for that,' said Ellie.

'We can call the police,' said Adam.

'I have another idea,' said Adam. 'There are lots of bushes here and we can't see much. Let's walk on the path where we can see down the cliff, and then maybe we can see Sam.'

'OK. I want to stay here at the top,' said Berry.

'OK. Luca, you stay here with Berry,' said Ellie. 'Adam, let's go on the path.'

'Why must I stay here?' asked Luca.

'Because it was MY idea,' said Adam.

'Yeah, but …,' said Luca.

'Give us ten minutes,' said Ellie.

'OK,' said Berry. 'Text when you know something.'

'Come on, Adam,' said Ellie. 'Let's go!'

Ellie and Adam ran on the path and around a corner. Then they came to a place at the top of the cliff where there weren't any bushes. There was just a small fence. The kids stopped. They could see some of the cliff.

'Look there are the bushes where Berry and Luca are waiting,' said Ellie.

'Yeah, but I can't see Sam,' said Adam.

'No, I can't see him,' said Ellie. 'Oh dear, this isn't good. I must tell Berry.'

Ellie started to write a text.

'Wait a minute,' said Adam. 'I think I saw something move over there but maybe it was just a big rabbit.'

'I don't think rabbits live on cliffs or near cliffs,' said Ellie. 'Where did you see it?'

'Over there, in the grass,' said Adam.

Then suddenly Adam was very excited.

'It IS Sam!' he shouted. 'He's OK.'

Ellie looked and then she was very excited too.

'Yes, now I can see him,' she shouted. 'What does he have? What's there? Maybe it's a person and they're hurt ...'

'... or dead!' said Adam.

Adam and Ellie were both very quiet for a moment.

'I must send Berry a text,' said Ellie.

Come quick!! We C Sam. He's OK but has sth.

Ellie's mobile beeped.

We're coming!! ☺☺☺☺

Berry and Luca came to Ellie and Adam. Luca was pushing Berry in her wheelchair really fast.

'Careful, Luca, not too fast!' shouted Ellie when she saw them. 'Berry doesn't want to go down the cliff!'

'Ha, ha!' shouted Luca. 'Don't worry.'

'Where's Sam?' said Berry when she and Luca got to the fence where Ellie and Adam were.

'Over there,' said Ellie. 'Can you see him?'

'Yes,' said Berry. 'He has something, you're right. It looks like a bag but I'm not sure.'

Berry started to wave and shout.

'Sam, come here!' she shouted.

Sam looked up but he stayed there.

'Why doesn't he come back up the cliff?' said Adam.

'I don't know,' said Berry.

'I think somebody fell down the cliff and now they're dead,' said Adam. 'Sam is staying with him or her.'

'Adam, you watch too many detective films on TV,' said Berry.

'No, I don't,' said Adam. 'Terrible things happen on the cliffs every day.'

'Not every day,' said Ellie.

'Let's find out what Sam has' said Luca. 'I can go down the cliff. It's easy.'

Suddenly, he went over the fence and down onto the cliff.

'Luca, come back!' shouted Ellie. 'It's too dangerous!'

Luca started to climb down the cliff but then he suddenly stopped. 'It's scary!'

He climbed back over the fence and onto the path.

'That was a bad idea,' said Luca. 'What now?'

'I have an idea,' said Berry.

She took a box of biscuits out of her backpack and then shook it hard. Then she shouted:

'Sam! Come here! Come here NOW!'

At first, Sam just looked at Berry and wagged his tail. Then she shook the box of biscuits again. The kids watched Sam. He had something in his mouth and started to climb up the cliff.

'Hurray!' they all shouted. 'Come on, Sam!'

'What is he bringing with him?' said Luca.

'It looks like a bag. Sam likes to find things,' said Berry.

'So it isn't a dead person?' asked Adam.

'No, Adam,' laughed Luca. 'It's just a bag.'

'Sam is really good at climbing the cliff. He's not scared like you' said Adam.

'Come on, Sam!' shouted Berry. 'Good boy! Come on!'

Sam climbed up the cliff to the fence.

'Good boy,' said Berry. 'Give me that bag.'

Sam climbed through the fence with the bag in his mouth and when Berry hugged Sam, he dropped the bag on the ground and wagged his tail.

Adam took the bag and opened it.

'What are you doing?' said Luca. 'It isn't your bag.'

'Maybe there's a treasure in it,' said Adam.

'Ha, ha,' said Luca.

Sam wagged his tail and looked at Adam.

## Chapter 6

The three kids looked at Adam. He still had the bag. They were all very quiet. Berry was the first to say something.

'I think Luca is right,' she said. 'It isn't our bag, so don't open it, Adam.'

'But we have to open it' said Ellie. 'Then we can find out who it belongs to and then we can give it back.'

'Hmmm, maybe Ellie's right,' said Luca.

'Well, someone threw the bag over the cliff so maybe they don't want it,' said Ellie.

'But there's something in it,' said Adam.

'Well, OK, let's see what's inside,' said Berry. 'Maybe rubbish.'

'No, it's a treasure,' said Adam.

They all laughed.

'OK, so what's in the treasure bag, Adam?' said Berry.

Adam opened the bag and looked inside.

'Er…well, there's this,' said Adam.

He took a sandwich out of the bag and showed it to everybody.

'That isn't very interesting,' said Ellie.

'Is that all, an old sandwich?' said Luca.

Adam looked at the date on it.

'It has tomorrow's date on it,' said Adam, 'so it isn't old.

Sam wagged his tail and then sat and looked at Adam.

'So that's what was interesting for Sam,' laughed Ellie.

'Can I give it to him, Berry?' asked Adam.

'Yes, OK,' said Berry.

Adam gave the sandwich to Sam.

'Is there anything else in the bag?' asked Berry.

'Yeah, something cool,' said Luca.

Adam looked in the bag again.

'Hmmm, I think there's only a boring towel,' he said.

'Well, take it out,' said Ellie. 'Maybe there's something else in there.'

As Adam took the towel out of the bag, something fell on the grass.

'What's that?' asked Berry. 'Something was in the towel.'

Luca picked up a camera.

'It's a small camera,' he said. 'It looks like an expensive one but I don't know much about cameras.'

'I do,' said Adam. 'Let me look at it.'

Luca gave the camera to Adam.

'Wow, cool,' said Adam. He was very excited. 'I know all about this camera. You …'

'Adam, don't …' said Ellie.

But it was too late. Adam and Luca were looking at the photos in the camera.

'It's OK,' said Adam. 'Hmmm, nothing very interesting, just lots of pictures of the Hoe, the lighthouse and the Lido.'

'Maybe the camera belongs to a tourist,' said Ellie.

'Why did they throw the bag over the cliff?' said Berry.

Ellie picked up the bag and looked in it. On the inside of the bag, there were the letters 'A.W.'. Ellie showed the letters to Berry.

'Hmmm, so the bag belongs to "A.W.," said Berry. 'But that doesn't help us much. Who is "A.W."?'

Adam and Luca were still looking at the photos in the camera. Suddenly, Luca was very excited.

'Wow, that's mega cool!' he said. 'That's a really good photo of a police helicopter.'

'It looks like it's in the shopping zone,' said Adam. 'Maybe it's the one we saw today.'

'Yeah,' said Luca. 'Let's see the next photo.'

'What's interesting about helicopters?' said Ellie.

'It's a boy thing,' said Luca.

'No, it isn't only a boy thing,' said Berry.

'Yes, it is,' said Luca.

'No, it is NOT,' said Berry.

'Guys, shut up!' shouted Adam.

The others looked at Adam. His face was very white. Sam stopped wagging his tail.

'What's up, Adam?' asked Berry.

'Look at this photo,' Adam said quietly. He gave the camera to Berry. Luca and Ellie were behind her so that they saw the photo too.

In the photo there was a man and a lot of red all around him. A young woman with long brown hair was near the man. She had a big knife with blood on it in her hand.

The four kids looked at each other.

'It's a photo of a murder,' said Berry quietly.

## Chapter 7

'We have to go to the police,' said Berry. 'This is really serious.'

'That's why there were police helicopters and police cars,' said Adam. 'They were looking for the murderer.'

'Yeah,' said Luca. 'But why ...'

Suddenly, Berry's mobile beeped.

'It's a text from mum,' said Berry.

> Hi love, R U having a nice picnic? IM at hair salon in Drake Circus. B finished in 40 mins. Can meet U and ur friends 4 ice cream b4 home. Or dad can pick U up l8er? XX

'Mum is at Drake Circus,' said Berry. 'Let's go there and tell her about the murder.'

'Yeah, good idea,' said Ellie. 'Let's put the camera and the towel back into the bag and take it with us.'

'Or we could throw the bag back over the cliff,' said Luca.

'Luca!' said Berry, 'We can't do that.'

'It was just a joke,' said Luca.

'It wasn't very funny.' said Adam.

'No, it wasn't,' said Berry. Then she wrote a text to her mum.

> Gr8. On our way xx

The kids went quickly to Drake Circus. Ellie pushed Berry in her wheelchair, and the two boys pushed their bikes.

Sam ran next to Berry as she held onto his lead. The bag with the camera in it was on the back of Adam's bike.

'Guys, let's cross the road here and then go down New George Street,' said Berry. 'It's faster.'

'OK,' said Ellie. 'Good idea.'

As the kids and Sam waited to cross the road, a taxi went past them. A woman with long brown hair was looking out of the taxi's window. She looked at Sam and smiled.

Ellie saw the woman.

'Look!' shouted Ellie to the others. 'It's her!'

'Who?' asked Luca.

'Who are you talking about?' asked Berry.

'The murderer in the photo – she's in that taxi!' shouted Ellie. 'I saw her!'

The three kids looked at Berry. Then they watched as the taxi went down the road. Luca got on his bike.

'I can follow the taxi on my bike,' he said.

'And then ...?' said Berry. 'It's too dangerous.'

'Yeah, you're right,' said Luca.

'Well, the taxi is going too fast,' said Ellie.

'Are you sure it was the murderer?' asked Berry.

'Yes,' said Ellie.

'What a terrible woman,' said Adam. 'She's a murderer.'

'Well, what now?' asked Luca.

'We're really near Drake Circus,' said Berry. 'Let's ask mum. She always has an answer.'

When the kids arrived at the hair salon, the boys waited outside with Sam, and Berry and Ellie went in. The hairdresser was cutting Mrs Donovan's hair.

'Oh, hello, love. Hi Ellie,' said Berry's mum as soon as she saw the two girls.'

They looked at the hairdresser.

'Fifteen minutes,' she said.

'Oh,' said Berry's mum. 'Do you want to go to the ice cream shop and wait for me there?'

'Er ... yeah, OK,' said Berry.

'Are you OK, Berry?' said Berry's mum. 'You look a bit worried. What happened? Where's Sam?'

'Um ... don't worry, Mum. He's fine, he's outside with Luca and Adam,' said Berry.

'Good,' said Berry's mum. 'For a moment I thought something terrible happened on your picnic. Oh, do you remember this morning when all the roads to the shopping centre were closed and we were late for your picnic?'

For a moment, Berry's face went white.

'Yes,' said Berry.

'Well, I bought the *Herald* today,' said Berry's mum. 'Take it with you to the ice cream shop and look at it. It's in my bag. People think that nothing interesting happens in Plymouth but they're wrong.'

'Er ... OK, Mum,' said Berry. She took the newspaper from her mum's bag. 'See you in a minute.'

'OK, love,' said Mrs Donovan.

Berry and Ellie went to the boys. They were sitting on a bench near the hair salon. Adam was holding the bag with the camera in it. Sam wagged his tail as soon as he saw Berry.

'Did you tell your mum?' asked Luca.

'No, I didn't,' said Berry. 'The hairdresser is still cutting mum's hair. We can wait for her at the ice cream shop. She gave me the *Herald* and said there's something interesting in it.'

Berry put the newspaper on the bench.

'Yeah, old people love newspapers,' said Adam.

'Oh, no!' said Luca. 'I forgot to buy the *Herald* for dad.'

'There's a murderer here in Plymouth and you're worried about a stupid newspaper?' said Ellie.

'Yeah, we didn't even write down the number plate of the taxi,' said Adam. 'They always do that in detective stories and films.'

'Oh, Adam, this isn't a film,' said Ellie. 'This is real.'

'We still don't know who threw the bag over the cliff, who "A.W." is, or who the camera belongs to,' said Luca.

'No, and someone saw the murder because they took the photo,' said Ellie.

'What a mess,' said Berry. 'And now we're waiting for Mum and the only thing we have is this stupid newspaper. Oh well, let's look at it,'

## Chapter 8

Berry looked at the first page of the *Herald*.

'Hmmm, here's something interesting for you, Adam,' said Berry.

'What is it?' asked Adam.

'Listen,' said Berry as she started to read out loud from the newspaper:

'For the next ten days, a film company is making a detective film here in Plymouth.'

'Mega cool,' said Adam.

'Yeah, that IS cool,' said Luca.

'Are there any pictures?' said Adam.

'Er… the report about the film is on page seven, so let's see,' said Berry as she opened the newspaper to read the report. Suddenly, she was very excited.

'That's amazing,' said Berry.

'What?' asked Ellie.

'Look!' said Berry as she gave the *Herald* to the others. 'Look at the photos in the report.'

Adam, Luca and Ellie looked at the newspaper and then suddenly Ellie was very excited.

'There's a picture of the murderer!' shouted Ellie.

'Yeah, and the dead man!' shouted Luca. He was very excited too.

'That means …?' asked Adam.

'They're actors,' said Berry, 'and the photo in the camera is a scene from the film!'

'That's why the streets were closed?' asked Luca.

'Yes,' said Berry.

'They were making a film,' said Luca.

'Be quiet, Luca,' said Ellie. 'I'm trying to read the report.'

'That's why we saw the police helicopters over the Hoe,' said Luca. 'They weren't real.'

'I thought they were real,' said Adam.

'Yeah, but they weren't,' said Luca.

Ellie put the *Herald* back on the bench.

'OK, guys, so now we know it isn't a real murder,' she said. But we still have to find out who the camera belongs to and give it back.'

'Maybe "A.W." is someone who is working on the film,' said Adam.

'Yes, but how can we find out where the film people are?' asked Luca.

'Hmmm, the report in the *Herald* said the film people are in Plymouth for the next four days,' said Ellie.

'That's right,' said Berry. 'Maybe mum has an idea. We can ask her.'

'Er ... Do we tell your mum about Sam and the cliff?' said Adam.

'No,' said Berry. 'We can tell mum we just found the bag in the bushes.'

'But what about the bag?' asked Adam.

'What do you mean?' asked Luca. 'We can give it back to the film people tomorrow.'

'Yeah, I know that,' said Adam. 'But can I take it home and bring it tomorrow?'

'Oh, er ... that's fine with me,' said Berry. 'What about you, guys?'

'Good idea,' said Ellie.

'Be careful with the camera,' said Luca.

Just then Berry's mum came out of the hair salon. Sam wagged his tail as soon as he saw her.

'There you are,' she said.

'Hi, Mum,' said Berry.

'I'm sorry I'm late,' said Mrs Donovan.

'That's OK, Mum,' said Berry.

'Yeah, we looked at your *Herald*,' said Adam.

'It was very interesting,' said Luca.

'You can have the newspaper,' Mrs Donovan said to Luca.

'Thank you!' said Luca.

The kids smiled at each other.

'They are making the film here because Plymouth is so famous,' said Mrs Donovan.

'Famous for what?' whispered Adam to Luca.

'Er ... the Mayflower ship?' whispered Luca back to Adam. 'You know, the ship that went to America from Plymouth before people called it America.'

'I know about the Mayflower. I'm not stupid,' whispered Adam.

'Now,' said Mrs Donovan, 'would you kids like to have an ice cream before I take Berry and Sam home?'

'Yes, please,' said the four kids together.

Sam wagged his tail.

## Chapter 9

At school the next day, the four kids met in the canteen.

'That tourist information website your mum showed us is really interesting,' said Luca as he ate a chip.

'And now we know the film people are at the Aquarium this afternoon,' said Berry. 'We can go there after school.'

'Where's the bag, Adam?' asked Ellie.

Adam stopped and put his hamburger on his plate. He looked really worried.

'Er … I don't know how to tell you this, guys, but I forgot it on the school bus,' he said.

Berry, Luca and Ellie looked at Luca. They were serious.

'What!' they shouted.

Then Adam smiled.

'Ha, ha,' he said. 'That was a joke. Don't worry. The bag and the camera are in my sports locker.'

'Adam,' said Ellie, 'Sometimes you're a real …'

'… pain?' said Adam.

'That was a good joke, Adam,' said Luca as he took one of Adam's chips.

'Hey!' said Adam. 'You have your own chips, Luca.'

The other three kids laughed.

'After school we can take the bus to the Aquarium,' said Berry.

'Yeah and find out who "A.W." is,' said Adam. 'Maybe he's a famous film director.'

The others laughed again.

As soon as school was finished, the four kids met at the bus stop outside Eggy. Ellie looked down the street.

'The bus is coming,' said Luca. 'I can see it.'

'I hope that I can get on this bus,' said Berry.

The red Plymouth city bus stopped at the bus stop. The bus driver saw Berry in her wheelchair and he opened a special door for her.

'Thank you,' she said to the driver. 'That's great. Some buses don't have a special door.'

'This is a new bus, love,' said the driver. 'The old buses aren't good for wheelchairs.'

About 20 minutes later the bus stopped on Hoe Road and the four kids got off the bus. When they were near the Aquarium, there were two policemen on the small bridge.

'I'm sorry,' said one of the policemen. 'A film crew are in the Aquarium. It's closed this afternoon.'

'But we must give this bag to one of the film crew,' said Adam.

'Yes,' said Berry. 'It's important.'

Berry told the policemen about the bag, the camera and the letters "A.W." The two policemen were very serious.

'I need to look in that bag,' said one of the policemen.

Adam opened the bag and the policeman took out the camera and looked at it.

'OK,' said the policeman. 'Let's see ...'

The policeman said something into his police radio and then looked at the kids.

'OK,' he said to them. 'Come with me and bring the bag with you.'

The kids went with the policeman over the small bridge and when they were in front of the Aquarium, a young man was there to meet them. He had headphones and a microphone on.

'Thank you,' said the young man to the policeman. 'I can take them back over the bridge later.'

'OK, sir,' said the policeman.

As the policeman walked back over the bridge, the young man looked at the kids and smiled.

'Hello,' he said. 'My name is Oliver. Can I help you?'

'Hi,' said Berry. 'We're looking for someone and we think they're working on the film. Their first name starts with 'A' and their last name starts with 'W'. We have something that belongs to them.'

'Hmmm' said Oliver. "A.W."? Well, that's Alex Wingate. Alex does the stunts.'

'Stunts?' said Berry.

'Well,' said Oliver. 'In the film, the actors don't fly the police helicopters because they don't know how and it's too dangerous. So Alex flies them.'

'Mega cool!' said Luca and Adam together.

Oliver smiled again.

'Come with me,' he said.

The kids went with Oliver to the back of the Aquarium. Suddenly, the four kids were very excited. They saw a police helicopter and some people standing near it. They could also see film cameras and special film lights.

'Wow,' said Adam. 'This is amazing.'

'Look, there's the murderer ... I mean the actor who plays the murderer,' whispered Ellie.

'Where?' said Berry.

'She's over there with cup of tea,' said Ellie.

'Is that the film director talking to the camera person?' Adam asked Oliver.

'Yes,' said Oliver.

'There isn't much happening,' said Luca. 'Everybody is just standing and talking.'

'Well, it's hard to make a film so people have to talk about it a lot,' said Oliver smiling. 'Wait here, guys.'

The kids watched Oliver as he went to talk to a young woman. Then she and Oliver walked over to the kids.

'This is Alex,' said Oliver.

'Hi, guys,' said Alex.

Ellie and Berry smiled but the boys were serious.

'Your name is Alex, but...you're a woman!' said Luca.

'Yes, I am,' smiled Alex. 'Alex is for Alexandra, but my friends call me Alex.'

'And you fly the helicopter?' asked Adam.

'Yes,' said Alex, 'I do. That's my job.'

'See,' said Berry to Luca. 'It isn't just a boy's thing.'

'You're right,' Luca said.

'You found my bag?' asked Alex.

'Yes' said Adam as he gave the bag to Alex.

She opened it and took the camera and the towel out.

'Thank you so much,' said Alex.' Where was it?'

The kids told Alex everything. Then Alex told the kids someone stole the bag while she was in a cafe on the Hoe.

'Was there anything else in the bag?' asked Berry.

'Well, there was a purse in the bag with some money in it,' said Alex.

'Maybe the thief saw the purse and didn't think there was anything else in the towel,' said Ellie.

'Yes,' said Alex. 'The purse isn't very important, but there was also a nice cap in the bag. I guess the thief liked it too.'

'We didn't see a cap,' said Luca.

'I bought it when I was working on a film in California,' said Alex. 'It was my favourite San Francisco 49ers cap with an autograph from one of the team.'

'The 49ers?' said Adam.

'They're an American football team,' said Ellie.

Adam and Luca looked at Berry.

'How do you know?' said Luca.

'I know lots of things,' said Ellie.

Alex smiled.

'I have to talk to the film director soon,' she said. 'Can I see you guys again and do something nice to thank you, maybe at the weekend?'

The kids looked at each other and then Berry spoke:

'Yes, great,' she said. 'How can we contact you?'

Alex gave them her mobile number, and the four kids gave Alex their numbers. Then Oliver came to talk to Alex.

'Sorry,' he said. 'The film director needs you now.'

'Thanks, Oliver,' said Alex. Then she looked at the kids. 'Call me, OK?'

'OK,' said Berry. 'It was so great to meet you.'

'OK, guys' said Oliver. 'I can take you back over the bridge now.'

## Chapter 10

The next day after school, Adam helped in the cafe because it was really busy. He helped his mum make sandwiches. Then he cleaned the tables and took the dirty cups and plates into the cafe's kitchen. As he was in the kitchen, his mobile beeped.

Hi Adam, I'm in the cafe. R U here? Ellie

Adam then sent Ellie a text.

Yes, Gr8! C U in 1 min

'Mum, can I have a break?' asked Adam. 'Ellie is in the cafe.'

'Yes, love,' said Adam's mum. 'No problem. Take something drink and give Ellie a drink too.'

'Thanks, Mum,' said Adam.

He took two bottles of orange juice and then went to Ellie. She was sitting at a table outside the cafe and was looking at her mobile.

'Would you like an orange juice?' said Adam.

Ellie looked up and laughed.

'Yes, please,' she said.

'What are you doing, homework?' smiled Adam.

'Yeah, that's what my dad thinks,' said Ellie.

Adam sat next to Ellie. They were drinking their orange juice and talking. Suddenly, Ellie saw a man sit down at one of the tables. He wore a black T-shirt and blue jeans, and a cap. Ellie looked at the cap. It had the words 'San Francisco 49ers' on it, and it had an autograph on it.

'Adam!' Ellie whispered to Adam. 'I think that man has Alex's cap!'

Adam looked at the man.

'Yeah, and I know who he is,' whispered Adam. 'His name is Frankie and he's always in trouble with the police. He stole a bag from someone in the cafe. What can we do?'

'We must tell Alex,' said Ellie.

'Good idea,' said Adam. 'I have another idea too.

Adam picked up his mobile phone and quickly took a photo of Frankie.

'Look, you can see the 49ers cap and the autograph,' said Adam as he showed Ellie the photo.

'Cool,' said Ellie. 'Let's send the photo to Alex now.'

Suddenly, Frankie got up from his table. Adam and Ellie watched him go out of the cafe. Then Adam sent the photo and a text message to Alex:

> Hi Alex, we think we know who stole your bag.
> Call when U can.

Then Adam's phone beeped.

'Answer your phone!' said Ellie. 'Maybe it's Alex.'

Adam looked at his mobile.

'It is! You answer it,' said Adam as he gave it to Ellie.

Ellie took Adam's mobile and told Alex about Frankie. Then Ellie put the mobile on the table.

'She wants to phone the police,' said Ellie. 'And she wants to meet us all on Saturday at 2 o'clock at the harbour!'

'Mega cool,' said Adam. 'Let's text the others and tell them!'

The next Saturday, Berry, Luca, Adam and Ellie went to the harbour and waited for Alex near the ice cream van. The kids were very excited.

'It's almost 2 o'clock,' said Adam.

Just then Alex got there.

'Hi guys,' she said. 'Good to see you!'

'You have the 49ers cap!' said Ellie.

'Yeah,' said Alex. 'The police gave it back to me. They went to Frankie's flat and found my purse too. The police told me what happened. Frankie stole my bag, took out the purse and then quickly threw the bag over the cliff.'

'Then the coolest dog found it,' said Adam.

'Yep,' said Alex. 'And the coolest kids gave it back to me. I would love to thank you in a special way.'

The four kids smiled.

'And I have an idea. Are you all free tomorrow?'

The kids looked at each other and then looked at Alex and smiled.

'Good!' said Alex. 'Do you want to go up in the police helicopter we use in the film?'

'Yes, please!' said Berry and Ellie.

'Mega cool,' shouted Luca and Adam.

'And then you can all meet the actors and see how we make the film,' said Alex.

'That's SO great,' said Berry, and the others nodded.

Then Alex looked at the ice cream van. The ice cream woman had the *Herald*.

'But let's have a big '99 Flake now,' said Alex.

'Yes!' shouted the kids. The kids were really loud. The ice cream woman smiled as soon as she saw Adam.

'A small '99 Flake?' she asked him.

'No, five big '99 Flakes, please!' he said.

Alex and the others laughed.

# Vocabulary

## A

**a lot** [ə lɒt] viel; viele; eine Menge
**amazing** [ə'meɪzɪŋ] unglaublich
**arrived** [ə'raɪvd:] **Then Adam and Luca arrived.** Dann kamen Adam und Luca an.
**as** [əz, betont æz] als
**as soon as** [əz suːn əz] sobald
**autograph** ['ɔ:togra:f] Autogramm

## B

**backpack** ['bækpæk] Rucksack
**Be careful** [bi 'keəfl] Sei vorsichtig/Pass auf
**beeped** [biːpt] **His mobile beeped.** Sein Handy piepte.
**belong to:** [bɪ'lɒŋ tə] **who it belongs to** wem es gehört
**bench** [bentʃ] Bank
**big wheel** [bɪg wiːl] Riesenrad
**bin** [bɪn] Mülltonne
**bought:** [bɔːt] **I bought the *Herald* today.** Heute kaufte ich den ‚Herald'.
**bush** [bʊʃ] Busch, Strauch

## C

**came:** [keɪm] **Luca's dad came into the kitchen.** Lucas Vater kam in die Küche.
**cap** [kæp] basecap
**caught:** [kɔːt] **He caught the frisbee.** Er fing den Frisbee.
**cliffs** [klɪfs] Klippen
**coolest:** [kuːlɪst] **the coolest dog** der coolste Hund
**company** ['kʌmpəni] **a film company** Filmgesellschaft
**cross the road:** [krɒs ðə rəʊd] **Let's cross the road here.** Lass uns hier die Straße überqueren.
**cut** [kʌt] (etwas) schneiden

## D

**dead** [ded] tot
**director** [də'rektə] Regisseur/in
**driver** ['draɪvə] Fahrer/in

## E

**each other:** [iːtʃ 'ʌðə] **The kids looked at each other.** Die Kinder schauten sich an.
**exciting** [ɪk'saɪtɪŋ] spannend, aufregend

## F

**famous** ['feɪməs] berühmt
**fell down:** [fel daʊn] **Maybe he fell down the cliff.** Vielleicht ist der die Klippen hinuntergestürzt.

**fence** [fens] Zaun
**flew:** [fluː] **The helicopter flew over the Hoe.** Der Hubschrauber flog über den Hoe.
**forgot:** [fə'gɒt] **I forgot to buy the Herald.** Ich vergaß den ‚Herald' zu kaufen.
**found:** [faʊnd] **We found the bag.** Wir fanden die Tasche.
**full:** [fʊl] **I'm really full.** Ich bin richtig satt.
**funny** ['fʌni] lustig

## G

**gave:** [geɪv] **She gave the boys their ice cream.** Sie gab den Jungen das Eis.
**give** [gɪv] geben
**grass:** [grɑːs] **on the grass** auf dem Rasen

## H

**hair** [heə] Haar
**hairdresser** ['heədresə] Friseur/in
**hand** [hænd] Hand
**head** [hed] Kopf
**headphones** ['hedfəʊnz] Kopfhörer
**helicopter** ['helɪkɒptə] Hubschrauber
**hold:** [həʊld] **hold onto the lead** die Hundeleine festhalten
**hugged:** [hʌgd] **Ellie hugged Berry.** Ellie umarmte Berry.
**hurt:** [hɜːt] **He's hurt.** Er ist verletzt.

## J

**joke:** [dʒəʊk] **Is that a joke?** Ist das ein Witz?

## K

**knife** [naɪf] Messer

## L

**lead:** [liːd] **the dog's lead** die Hundeleine
**light** [laɪt] Licht
**locker:** ['lɒkə] **The camera is in my locker.** Die Kamera ist in meinem Schließfach.
**long** [lɒŋ] lang
**loud:** [laʊd] **a loud noise** ein lautes Geräusch

## M

**mess:** [mes] **What a mess.** Was für ein Durcheinander.
**met:** [met] **They met in the canteen.** Sie trafen sich in der Kantine.
**microphone** ['maɪkrəfəʊn] Mikrofon
**murder** ['mɜːdə] Mord
**murderer** ['mɜːdərə] Mörder/in

## N

**number plate** ['numbə pleɪt] Nummernschild

## P

**path** [pɑːθ] Fußpfad
**police** [pə'liːs] Polizei

**purse** [pɜːs] Geldbeutel
**put:** [pʊt] **They put their books in their bags.** Sie steckten ihre Bücher in ihre Taschen.

**R**

**ran:** [ræn] **Sam ran to Ellie.** Sam rannte zu Ellie.
**report:** [rɪ'pɔːt] **reports in the newspaper** Berichte in der Zeitung
**robber** ['rɒbə] Räuber/in
**rubbish** ['rʌbɪʃ] Müll/Abfall

**S**

**saw:** [sɔː] **She saw a great place.** Sie sah eine tollen Stelle.
**serious:** ['sɪəriəs] **The police were serious.** Die Polizisten waren ernst.
**shook:** [ʃʊk] **She shook the box of biscuits.** Sie schüttelte die Schachtel Hundekekse.
**shout** [ʃaʊt] schreien; nach jmdm. rufen
**sirens:** ['saɪrənz] **police sirens** Polizeisirenen
**smile** [smaɪl] lächeln
**special:** ['speʃl] **He opened a special door.** Er öffnete eine Tür mit Rollstuhlzugang.
**started:** [stɑːtɪd] **Ellie started to write.** Ellie fing an zu schreiben.
**still:** [stɪl] **There is still a bit of cake.** Es gibt noch ein bisschen Kuchen.
**stole** [stəv] klaute
**strong** [strɒŋ] stark
**suddenly** ['sʌdənli] plötzlich

**T**

**take the dog for a walk** [teɪk] den Hund spazieren führen
**that's why:** [ðæts waɪ] **That's why I like living here.** Deshalb wohne ich hier so gerne.
**threw:** [θruː] **She threw a Frisbee.** Sie warf ein Frisbee.
**thought:** [θɔːt] **I thought something terrible happened.** Ich dachte, etwas Schreckliches sei passiert.
**told:** [təʊld] **Berry told the policeman about the bag.** Berry erzählte dem Polizisten von der Tasche.
**tomorrow:** [tə'mɒrəʊ] **Are you free tomorrow?** Hast du morgen Zeit?
**took:** [tʊk] **She took a cake out of her backpack.** Sie nahm einen Kuchen aus ihrem Rucksack.
**treasure:** ['treʒə] **Maybe there is a treasure in the bag.** Vielleicht ist ein Schatz in der Tasche.

**V**

**van:** [van] **Ice cream van** Eisverkaufswagen

## W

**wagged his tail:** [wægd hɪz teɪl] **Sam wagged his tail.** Sam wedelte mit dem Schwanz.

**wave:** [weɪv] **Berry started to wave and shout.** Berry fing an zu winken und zu rufen.

**went:** [went] **They went to the window.** Sie gingen zum Fenster.

**What's up?** [wɒts ʌp] Wie geht's? Was ist los?

**whisper** ['wɪspə] flüstern

**white:** [waɪt] **Berry's face went white.** Berry wurde kreidebleich.

**wore:** [wɔː] **He wore a T-shirt.** Er trug ein T-Shirt.

## Check your understanding

### Chapter 1

1 What do Berry, Ellie, Luca and Adam want to do on the weekend?

2 When do they want to meet?

### Chapter 2

1 What does Luca's father want Luca to buy when he's with Berry, Ellie and Adam?

2 Why was Luca late?

3 What do Luca and Adam see in the sky as they eat their ice cream?

### Chapter 3

1 Who is Sam?

2 What does Berry want to do with Sam later?

### Chapter 4

1 What game do the kids and Sam play?

2 What does Berry put on Sam when they want to take him for a walk?

3 What does Sam run after when he runs away?

## Chapter 5

1 Who goes on the path to look for Sam?

2 Where does Adam see Sam?

3 Why does Sam come back up the cliff?

4 What does Sam have in his mouth when he comes back up the cliff?

## Chapter 6

1 What things are in the bag?

2 Who does the bag belong to?

3 What sorts of photos do the kids see on the camera?

## Chapter 7

1 Why does Adam think the police helicopters were flying around Plymouth?

2 Where do the kids go to meet Berry's mum?

3 What does Berry's mum give to her?

## Chapter 8

1 What information does Berry find out about in the *Herald?*

2 What photo does Berry see on page 7?

3 Why were the streets really closed?

4 Who's 'A.W.'?

## Chapter 9

1 Where do the kids go to find 'A.W.' ?

2 What's Alex Wingate's job?

3 What isn't in the bag?

## Chapter 10

1 Who visits Adam in his mum's cafe?

2 Where did they see the 49ers cap?

3 Who's Frankie?

4 Who stole Alex's bag?

5 What do Berry, Luca, Ellie and Adam do with Alex the next day?